Grieve God's Way

Step By Step Guide

I0423365

Dr. Christine Rice Slocumb

Grieve God's Way is designed to help pastors, lay ministers, hospitals, doctors office, and other corporate organizations to set up a bereavement department or programs within their local church or business to effectively help those who grieve.

EARLY PRAISE FOR GRIEVE GOD'S WAY

Angels All Around Us

When Sara, my sister asked me to support her by coming with her to these grief classes, I thought "oh my goodness we will just sit around and cry and talk about our loved ones like they now can walk on water. And if I made it through one class, I just didn't know if I could make it through all four. Imagine my surprise when I realized I was looking forward to going to these classes.

The meditation and music were awesome!! It should be done in every class. For those who do meditate, it was a special gift in class. For those who do not meditate, it was another tool to use in time of need.

I wish there was a cd to take home.

The art class, again, another tool or outlet if you will. The subconscious never lies and can bring forth things we need to work on. I never did an art class before this way and found it to be a great way of expression, a way to start to talk. In my prayers at night, I pray this class continues forever, and that every physician's office had some kind of information about this.

Christine this letter would not be complete without me thanking you. And just so you know, I do believe in angels on earth, and I know you are one! The need is great. Again, I have received without asking…God led us to you, He is great! I will never forget these classes nor the experience.

-Felecia A. H.

I Will Smile Again

My sessions have been such an experience. No words can explain the peace, joy, love I feel. First I cried, I could not talk, but every

Tuesday I cried less and talked more.

By the session on music, I found myself knowing I could move forward without regrets and one day without tears, I will smile again. Every day a wonderful day to look forward to. Alone, yet not alone.

Painting my picture released me of my pain and suffering.

Today is the first day of the rest of my life and it is a good day. Praise God, These sessions allowed me to be released and move on to be happy, which is what my husband Howard would have wanted. The gift that God and Christine have given me is a peace that passes all understanding. **— Sarah H.**

I'm Alive!! Colors all bright & beautiful. That is what I saw through the guided imagery class. The grief in my soul exploded and left me alive. Before the classes I was contemplating suicide, even during the class thoughts would come.

I missed my husband and daughter so much! But during the painting when my soul exploded inside of me, I found joy like never before, which left me alive! Thank you, Christine, Thank you, God.

— Carol S.

To Share or Not To Share?

Eight ladies in a room. Most can't talk because of the lumps in their throats. Why are we here? To grieve? It's not easy, but with the kind words spoken and encouragement. We begin to share our painful stories. How did Christine and Katie do it? There was only one answer. God put them here. They knew what to say and when to say it. We never felt pressured to speak, but soon most everyone begin to share their stories. I felt a heavy load being lifted off my heavy heart. I thought, these two ladies are so good at what they do; they are natural; love and God put them in our lives at the exact time we needed to realize some of our emotions.

I thank God for them. **— Isabelle R**

DEDICATION

This work is dedicated to the Father, Son, and Holy Spirit. Without the work of the Trinity working on my behalf where would I be? To my Godsent husband Ronnie, who is always encouraging, supporting and reminding me that we serve a great big God!

I would like to acknowledge my sister in Christ, Dr. Cathy Lorraine Bagley for all her advice and support. Your words are always motivating and uplifting. You are always willing to help and be a true friend, thank you

To everyone who has experienced or may be going through some form of grief in their life. Grief is not meant to take up residence within you. Let it go… Jesus has already carried the load.

CONTENTS

INTRODUCTION

Into each life, some rain will fall,

But that does not mean life will end.

We have a friend within ourselves;

And that is when life begins.

A broken heart will mend in time,

Just as flowers bloom;

And the sun will shine with radiant light;

As the storm clouds are removed.

So let the rain come tumbling down.

Let the teardrops fall.

Our Father God knows everything,

And He will heal the heart.

Note to the Ministry. Grief God's Way is designed with you in mind to provide families and individuals with creative ways to express their grief and move beyond the death of a loved one and other losses.

Within the body of Christ, it seems that Christians suffer a bit more from the aftermath of grief and bereavement than those in the world. Not to say that those in the world should suffer more by no means, but for those of us who are followers of Christ Jesus, we should know that we could go through our grief a bit easier because God gives us the grace to walk through things differently. It does not mean that we will not feel the pain of the loss; it just means we have the grace and strength of almighty God to rest upon.

With everything that is going on in the world today, people are experiencing so much grief. We live in a place where morals and values seem to have left this generation of people. If the church is not equipped to handle grief that a person may experience from every aspect, then the lives of many will be lost, be it from suicides or murders. In today's society many are looking to fill an empty space, a void, a hole in their heart that only Jesus Christ can fill, therefore the church is supposed to be the one place a person can go to seek refuge.

When addressing the topic of grief & bereavement, one must understand that bereavement is associated only with the death of a loved one. Grief comes from the fact that the loved one has died. A person can also experience grief through other losses such as; divorce, loss of limbs, job, domestic violence, youth violence, loss of a home; and much more.

In (Matthew 11:28-30) God's word tells us to "Come to Him all you who labor and are heavy laden, and I will give you rest. He tells us; Take My yoke upon you and learn from Me; for I am gentle and lowly in heart, and you will find rest for your souls. He continues to assure us; for My yoke is easy and My burden is light."

In the corporate world of counseling with families and individuals who experience death and dying, grief and bereavement, one must be very careful not to use the name of Jesus when helping a family. America, although founded upon Christianity has now turned into a nation where everyone has their own religion and beliefs, and their own gods. Jesus has to take a back seat; that is of course, in the worldly system.

As Christians, we know that our thinking about death and dying, grief and bereavement should be based upon solid biblical ground. So the question is this: How does God in Scripture define death? First, the Scripture gives us a distinction between physical death and spiritual death.

The Bible speaks of the two distinctly, but they share one common characteristic. The Biblical definition of death - whether physical or spiritual - is not to be nonexistence, but separation. Physical death is the separation of body and soul. "Then the dust will return to the earth as it was, and the spirit will return to God who gave it" (Ecclesiastes 12:7).

Spiritual death means that man, apart from salvation in Christ, is separated from God. All who were sinners in Adam died in Adam, just as all who are justified in Christ are made alive in Christ (1 Corinthians 15:22). The final state of unsaved souls cast into the lake of fire for eternity is called "the second death" in the book of Revelation chapter 21:8.

It is understandable that God put the doctors here for us and that there is a clinical side to counseling. The point I am trying to make is that one cannot function without the other. In order to combat grief, bereavement and other losses, spiritual and clinical counseling must work hand in hand. Some would beg to differ; but it is only with the help of the Father, Son and Holy Spirit working on a person's behalf, can one truly recover from grief and receive total healing and restoration; be it physical or spiritual.

This handbook is uniquely put together to meet the need of the ministry within a church setting and help those who are experiencing death and dying, grief and bereavement. Sample letters and forms are included to give you an idea on how to personalize God's ministry.

This handbook designed is to provide families and individuals with creative ways to express their grief and move beyond the death of a loved one and other losses. Often times within the church body laborers are few; therefore, it creates an environment where provision through outreach ministry is limited to reach those who are grieving.

Of course, there are the deacons and other laypersons within the church, but often times it's still not enough to reach the multitudes of families that are in need of help and perhaps to prevent someone from harming themselves and others or those thinking about suicide while dealing with their loss.

There are several ways to implement a grief and bereavement ministry. Some churches actually have chaplains and counselors as members who are able to provide the service. Some use a referral system by utilizing professional Christian counselors within the community, who may only charge a sliding scale fee, based on client's income. Others decide to have a bereavement program set up within their church as part of the ministry.

In order to help someone who may be experiencing grief and bereavement, the person helping must understand the difference between the two. This handbook will guide you systematically and help you set up bereavement services within your local congregation.

This handbook is not to replace services that one may need within a hospital or hospice setting. It serves merely to come alongside to assist and impart basic knowledge and wisdom when ministering to those who are grieving.

As you minister to those who are grieving, please keep in mind that everyone's grief journey is distinctive; no one person will grieve the same way.

May God bless you as you continue to bless others and may you have an awesome forever.

1. **WHO WE ARE**

This is an area where you let the members of your congregation or others know about the grief services you will provide. (Where the blank spaces are just plug in your ministry name).

(Your name here) Grief & Bereavement Services is a wide-ranging grief resource program where we provide to families and individuals spiritual, clinical and emotional support to help them overcome all fragments of hurt and pain to move beyond death and other losses.

We reach out to comfort and encourage those who are confined to their homes, hospitals and other healthcare facilities due to illness or other medical conditions. If a loved one is under the care of Hospice, (Your name here) Grief & Bereavement services will come alongside and offer help.)

Should your family suffer a death, we stand ready to serve and assist with funeral arrangements and other details.

If your family or you as an individual suffer other losses such as divorce, loss of job, home, etc. (Your name here) Grief & Bereavement services will give support while recovery from your loss takes place.

We offer group and individual counseling, reminiscing activities, and educational information to families in need of support.

We connect with families and develop firm relationships, as we understand their stories to help provide them with the best support to meet their need.

We place families in our programs, refer them to outside organizations or to individuals that can provide additional services that we may not be able to accommodate.

All of our services are provided by experienced certified grief counselors, as well as volunteers who have been trained to understand the Grief & bereavement field.

(Your name here) Grief & Bereavement Services are provided at no cost but family members are asked to make a donation to help support the bereavement ministry. If a family cannot donate; (Your name here) Grief & Bereavement Services will still provide for you.

(Your name here) Grief & Bereavement Service aim is to maintain an atmosphere of compassion and love where families can find ongoing support and healing as they journey through their grief.

This will be accomplished through (Your name here) mailings of inspirational newsletters, cards, etc... As well as follow-up phone calls and home visits.

(Your name here) Grief & Bereavement Service Counselors will have scheduled team meetings to monitor and determine the best plan of care for individuals and families who are grieving.

2. GRIEF & BEREAVEMENT DEFINED

The Value of Wisdom and Knowledge Proverbs 2:1-10

"My son if you receive my words.
And treasure my commandments within you,
So that you incline your ear to wisdom,
And apply your heart to understanding;
Yes, if you cry out for discernment,
And lift up your voice for understanding,
If you seek her as silver,
And search for her as for hidden treasures;
Then you will understand the fear of the Lord,
And find the knowledge of God.
For the Lord gives wisdom;
From His mouth come knowledge and understanding;
He stores up sound wisdom for the upright;
He is a shield to those who walk uprightly;
He guards the paths of justice,
And preserves the way of His saints.
Then you will understand Righteousness and justice,
Equity and every good path.
When wisdom enters your heart,
And knowledge is pleasant to your soul.

What Is Bereavement?

Bereavement is associated with the death of loved one. It is what a person goes through when someone close to them dies. When that person dies, it begins the journey of grief.

What is Grief?

Grief: The emotional natural reaction to any loss. Grief deals with more than just a death of a loved one. Everyone experiences some form of grief in his or her life.

Anticipatory Grief: Grief that strikes in advance of an approaching loss. The person may feel anticipatory grief for a loved one who is sick and dying. Anticipatory grief gives the individual and loved one time to prepare and the ability to put things in place leading up to the loss, as they are grieving.

Grieving: A personal experience; it is the process of emotional and life adjustments you go through after any kind of loss. Depending on whom you are and the nature of your loss, the grieving will be different from another person's experience. There is no right or wrong way to grieve nor is there a time to tell a person how long they must grieve. Individual experiences of grief vary and are influenced by the nature of the loss.

Mourning: The outward expression of loss and grief. Mourning includes rituals and other actions that are specific to each person's culture, personality, and religion. Bereavement and mourning are both part of the grieving process.

Who Is The Bereaved?

The bereaved is a person who has sorrow through loss or deprivation of any kind.

Who Is The Loved One?

The loved one is the deceased, meaning; the person who has died.

What Is Death And Dying?

Physical death: The separation of body and soul. Man is a spirit, who possess a soul and lives in a body. "Then the dust will return to the earth as it was, and the spirit will return to God who gave it.

Spiritual death means that man, apart from salvation in Christ, is separated from God.

Dying: When someone is near death; their mind and each vital organs of the physical body will begin to shut down gradually and can build up over time.

What Are Other Losses?

Other losses consist of divorce, loss of limbs, loss of freedom, natural disasters, job, home, pet, friendship, etc...

Basic Bereavement Questions:

Q - Does a person only grieve death?

A - No, we grieve all losses.

Q - Do only family members grieve?

A - No, everyone who is attached to the deceased or other losses grieves.

Q - Should people stay at home while grieving?

A – It depends on the individual person but grief is not bound to a place and time.

Q - Should people be left alone while grieving?

A – It depends on the individual person but often times the griever needs to tell their story to someone.

5. How long does it take to recover from grief?

Grief has no time period and each person is different.

Summary of Bereavement Facts:

Over time, people learn to live with their losses. Grief is an emotional reaction and is manifested in many ways. Children grieve too, but they process it differently in their mind than adults. Some examples of loss include the death of a loved one, the ending of an important relationship, job loss, loss through theft or the loss of independence through disability or imprisonment.

When people talk about their grief, it brings healing. If a person has experienced the loss of a loved one, family member or friend or if a traumatic event which has changed their life, they will experience mourning and grief. The grieving journey allows time to reflect and find the strength to continue life and move forward. A person has the right to experience their own unique grief. No one person will grieve the same way.

Grief brings a multitude of emotions, confusion, disorientation, fear, guilt and relief are just a few of the emotions a person may feel.

Not all bereaved need to be taken care of due to the fact they were prepared mentally, spiritual, and had planned financially for such a time. Only with the help of the Father, Son and Holy Spirit working on a person's behalf can one truly recover from grief.

3. ESTABLISHING GRIEF MINISTRY

Unity, 1 Corinthians 12:4; 7

There are diversities of gifts, but the same Spirit.

There are differences of ministries,

But the same Lord.

And there are diversities of activities,

But it is the same God who works all in all.

But the manifestation of the Spirit

Is given to each one for the profit of all;

Within the church, there is a wide diversity of gifts, but the same spirit. Each person has been gifted to contribute something necessary to the body of Christ to enhance one's life while building up The Kingdom of God.

Gather together a team within your church community who truly has a heart for death, dying and loss; call a meeting and decide if the ministry will only support those who have lost a loved one due to death. Or will the ministry help those with other losses such as; relationships, jobs, loss of limbs, divorce etc., and then divide the responsibilities.

A few other things to consider is the differences between state-licensed professional counselors and Christian counselors. The state -licensed professional counselor is prohibited to pray, read or refer to the Holy Scripture, counsel against things such as abortion, homosexuality, etc. State-licensed counselors must not promote their personal religious beliefs. The only time a state-licensed counselor can involve religious (Christian) principles, morals, activities, instruction, etc., is if the person they are counseling initiates or requests counsel in this area.

The state-licensed counselor may not have the education, experience and knowledge of Scripture that the Christian counselor provides. Also, the Christian counselor may not have the experience as the state-licensed; therefore they should be able to work together and help each other in areas of lack.

Put guidelines in place for funerals, and grief support groups as well as individual counseling. Since you are the church and man is a spirit who possess a soul and lives in a body, healing of the whole body should be a foremost part of the church.

Check within your community and surrounding areas to see what other resources are available and perhaps networking can be established.

From that point, decide when other meetings will be held to evaluate the program's effectiveness once in place. Next, begin to educate and provide training for your team.

Those who already have training and experience in grief and bereavement and other losses can and should serve as mentors. The type of training offered for the team will depend on the person who is in the leadership position of the Bereavement Ministry; bereavement training may vary.

4. HOW TO HELP THOSE WHO GRIEVE

This Too Shall Pass

We don't know your struggle;
But we want you to know God is able.
To put joy back in your heart
In case things should fall apart.
We don't know your struggle
But we can feel your pain
Share with you in your journey
Cover you in the rain.
We don't know your struggle
But if you let us, we will try
To understand the words
Behind the tears that you may cry
We don't' know your struggle
But there is someone who does
He sends His guardian angels
To watch over all of us.

Pastoral care, grief support groups or individual counseling can help; but more importantly, time is the best factor. It is at this point where an assessment of the individual or family will need to be addressed.

A bereavement assessment will help determine the bereaved person's coping skills (normal, medium or high risk) depending on the risk, a bereavement plan of care will be implemented to meet the need.

Once a bereavement plan of care is put in motion, the individual or families healing journey can be monitored. As the bereaved improves or grief gets worse the bereavement plan of care can be adjusted.

Occasionally there may be an individual or family whose grief goes beyond what is being offered through your ministry. At this point, the person may need to be referred out for deeper counseling and or look into more of a clinical setting for a short period of time.

What To Look For When A Person Is Grieving?

There is such a wide range of feelings, emotions and symptoms that a person may experience when grieving. It has been said or adopted that there are stages of grieving. I tend to not call them stages because not all people who are grieving encounter the same thing; there is no formula to grief. As a person continues to move through life, feelings change as well as circumstances, which eventually will release a person from symptoms associated with grief. Through past experiences, I found that if the person grieving does not go through all the emotions, feelings or symptoms listed, they become so distraught and believe their reason for not healing quickly enough was due to some missing grief emotion. Remind the bereaved person that it is okay if they do or do not experience everything on the list.

Below is a list of emotions that a person may experience. Please note that any of these symptoms can happen to a person at anytime, anywhere and anyplace. This list may or may not apply to everyone:

Physical Symptoms: Include shortness of breath, loss of appetite, nausea, headaches, numbness, loss of sleep, and fatigue.

Emotional and Psychological Symptoms: Often involves confusion, shock, guilt, and self-blame, anger and denial. A need to retell the story of the loved one's death, dreams of the deceased, since the loved-one's presence. Emotions can consist of being anxious, restless, and nervous along with worry and suicidal thoughts. Desire to drink or use drugs, loneliness, longing, feelings of abandonment, relief, sadness, and vulnerability.

Things You Should Not Say To The Bereaved:

Most people do not have a clue what to say to someone who is grieving. So often times they may say things that are not helpful. Remember life and death are in the power of the tongue (Prov. 18:21) and the words we speak are spirit and life (John 6:63) therefore always approach the bereaved with tenderness.

When ministering to the bereaved, you may find that they may be angry at God and it is okay as long as the anger subsides. Grieving people have the right to search for meaning by asking why he or she died; Why did this happen to me; Why now; What did I do wrong; and so forth? Some questions may have answers and some may not.

Never tell a person who is grieving… "I know exactly how you feel." No, you can't know. Even if you've experienced a similar loss, you're not the bereaved person, and you didn't have the same relationship to the person who died.

Never tell a grieving person that it was God's will. I know, this is the "church", and its ministry, but depending on the relationship that person may have with God, it could cause more harm than good.

Never tell the bereaved that it's time to let go. Or that time heals all wounds. When helping someone through their pain they are the only ones who really know how they feel. Jesus is the only one that can heal the broken hearted and binds up all our wounds. (Psalm 147:3) He is the only one who knows the time.

Do not tell them to stop crying. Expressing strong emotions are normal healthy reactions to death and dying and other losses. Another no! no is to say "At least he/she is not suffering anymore." At this moment especially if they are not spiritually in tune, the person grieving will not fully understand those words.

This is one that is said a lot to a bereaved person. "You must be strong." (Or "God never gives us more than we can handle.") When a grieving person hears this, if they are not walking with God; what they hear from you is….it's wrong to feel grief. And they may think God is not with them because at this moment they are not strong.

Do not tell a grieving person "God must have wanted him/her." There again, unless the person grieving has a strong connection with God, attaching a spiritual significance to the loss could do more harm than good. "At least he/she was old enough to live a full life." It does not matter what the age was to someone who has lost a loved-one. Besides, how old would old enough be for someone who experience the death of a loved-one?

"You're lucky. At least you have money, you're young, God will send you someone else in time, or at least he/she didn't commit suicide. Those are not comforting words to speak; loss of any kind is always heartbreaking. Comparing misfortunes to others' or to alternate scenarios won't make the person feel better.

"It's been six months, one year, etc. it's time to move on." People never stop grieving the death of a loved one or other losses. Throughout their life, that person, place or thing will be with them. The grief will eventually develop into a settled remembrance of the loss. Meaning there may be times when they see, hear or do something that will trigger the mind of that loss. A deadline to mourning is insensitive and does little to help people learn to live through their loss. The clinical side of things would say 6 months is complicated grief and the bereaved should seek clinical help.

Within a church setting, you should find out what is truly the root issue causing the prolonged grief. For example, the bereaved may have guilt issues, forgiveness, anger, and so forth.

Remember grief is not just associated with the death of a loved one, therefore, a grief issue could develop from abuse of some kind, a demonic stronghold, insecure issues, the list can go on and on, perhaps generational curses. Yes, grief can run deeper than death. Once the root issue is dealt with there is a great possibility that the individual can then come to know Jesus Christ and deliverance can take place, and healing can begin.

Encouraging Those Who Grieve:

To say to someone grieving "I feel your pain," Shows an expression of empathy. Or "Would you like a hug?" Even though some people are not touchy-feeling, sometimes one touch is all they need to begin their grieving journey and be healed. Just as the woman with the issue of blood, she only needed to touch the hem of Jesus garment and she knew she would be made whole. As believers in Christ Jesus with

Holy Spirit working through us, we carry that same anointed to heal the sick, raise the dead, and cast out devils. When a person is grieved and they allow us to hug them they will feel the love and compassion of Christ Jesus.

"I'm sorry for your loss" is a good thing to say; it's direct, it's honest, and shows you care. Perhaps you could open the way for them to talk about their love-one by saying, "would you like to talk about it?" Then honor their response.

Saying nothing is very powerful. Sometimes the bereaved just need the presence of a person. Especially if you are a clergy; your presence means a lot to those who are grieving; even though you never say one word. Make sure your body language displays one of compassion, and relaxation so the bereaved does not think your visit is out of obligation and you are in a hurry to leave.

Is there anything I may get for you? Or how can I help you? These are all good questions. Just make sure whatever the request may be, you are able to make it happen. They are already in a grieving state and do not need any more disappointments.

Be observant, notice if the person grieving has a relationship with God. If they are open to talking about spiritual things then do so. If not have some material on death, dying and biblical insight. Let the bereaved know that you are going to leave some literature to help them.

Let the bereaved know that it's okay to cry; Jesus wept (John 11:33, 35) Encourage those grieving to attend a grief support group. Grief support groups work well; it allows them to share their story. It allows them to connect with others who have a similar loss. Healing and deliverance can happen on a personal level.

5. FUNERAL ARRANGEMENTS

Only a breath away

We don't know the hour

Nor do we know the day.

We all have to leave this earth,

It's not our place to stay.

Your loved one now has died

But remember life lives on.

One day you will meet them

In the new earth to come

To be absent from the body

Is to be present with the Lord

Their soul is now a resting place

With Jesus forevermore.

When connecting to the church's "Bereavement" Services to make funeral arrangements for a loved one, all requests should be directed to the Bereavement Ministry by contacting the person in charge and making an appointment. As the contact person speaks with the bereaved family, one priority should be to find out if all arrangements have been made. If not, find out if the family needs help in making arrangements selecting a funeral home and cemetery, also do they have funds to pay the funeral cost.

Next, find out what type of burial service they want to have. Complete a bereavement profile with as much information as you have, often times certain details have to be added later.

If there is a need, Bereavement Services should assist with helping organize the order of service, select appropriate scriptures and songs, offer referrals to funeral homes and cemeteries, and provide insight on what will take place on the day of the service. If the Bereavement Ministry is willing to assist with financial burdens of the bereaved, then it would be a good idea to make sure a bereavement hardship fund is set up within the ministry. All approved planning must go through the Pastor and or Co-Pastor of the church.

Different Type of Services:

It is an honor for the church "Bereavement" Ministry Department to serve families as they celebrate the life of their loved one. Most of the time elders, ministers, ushers, musicians, and sound technicians are available for each service conducted within the place of worship. Let the families know how many people the church accommodates. What time services are usually conducted and on what day Also, if services can be held in the AM / PM.

Traditional Service: A traditional Funeral is a service held to memorialize a deceased person with their body (casket) present. The service is usually held in a church and is formal. The funeral home of choice is usually present and serves as the ushers. The church often times will render the music and sound technicians and the Pastor does the eulogy.

Memorial Service: Here the term memorial service alters the Traditional service by honoring the deceased person with pictures, flowers, crosses, and a funerary urn (without the presence of a casket, body). The actual service can be as formal as a traditional service or as relaxed as a time of reflection and fellowship. (Your name here) "Bereavement" will provide elders and ministers upon request, with a 14-day notice.

Graveside Service: Graveside Services are small and intimate which take place literally at the cemetery. Families coordinate this option with the cemetery and funeral home of their choice. Special features of graveside services usually include an extremely brief service (5 to 15 minutes duration), the on-site funeral home staff and family, an observation of the initial stages of the burial. When requested, (Your name here) elders and ministers are in place to officiate, pray, share words of comfort and offer the final burial.

Funeral Home Service: A funeral home service takes place in the chapel of a local funeral home. Whenever the family chooses this option for the service, the funeral home staff assists the family with planning the service. Upon request, (Your name here) "Bereavement" will provide elders and ministers. The funeral home staff is required to contact the Bereavement Office at least 14 days prior to the service.

Wake/Viewing/Family: Often time's families like to honor their loved one with a "wake," "viewing" or "family hour." All three of these services take place at the funeral home and are generally informal and have a brief time set aside for remarks and prayer. Informal wake, there is not an officiating person present. At any point, members of the audience are welcome to come up to the front of the chapel and offer reflections or share one-on-one with the deceased person's family. A minister or funeral home staff member will be present to oversee the proceedings if needed.

- Formal Wake: Takes place in the chapel of the funeral home, with the body of the deceased person present for public viewing. The funeral home staff will arrange the type of service the family desires. With a 14-day's notice, (Your name here) Ministries Bereavement can provide an elder or minister to be present.

- A Public Viewing: Is an option some families choose to provide an opportunity for others to come to the funeral home to see the deceased person. This option allows persons who cannot attend the Traditional Funeral or memorial service a time of private reflection with their friend. This is a time where the family or (Your name here) Ministries "Bereavement" is not present.

- The Family Hour: A prearranged period of time that one or more family members are present at the funeral home to receive visitors. The funeral home staff arranges a "parlor," where family members sit in the same private room with their loved one's body. Visitors share a few intimate moments with the family; bonds are reconnected, memories are stirred and encouragement is shared one with the other. (Your name here) "Bereavement" elders and ministers are not present during this time unless requested by the family.

Encouragement Tribute: This personal expression comes from The Pastor of (Your name here) Ministries. Members of the congregation receive this personal memento which may be in letter form or some sort of token. It is read or given during the remarks portion of the home going service and given to the family.

Repass Meals: Are provided for the immediate family members. "A Repass", or the gathering, occurs directly after the burial or burial ceremony has taken place. This event sometimes is held at the home of the bereaved family or at the church.

This gives family and friends a chance to share a meal and reflect on stories about the loved one. It's the final journey of the actual burial which helps with accepting the fact that the loved one has died.

By this time usually the family is exhausted and the last thing they need to be worried about is preparing a meal for guest and other family members to eat.

6. GRIEF RELIEF

The Silence of God

The silence of God does not mean
He is not listening.
The silence of God does not mean
He has not heard your prayers.
The silence of God does not mean
He has abandoned you.
The silence of God does not mean
He does not care.
Contrary;
The silence of God means
He is in the process of shifting
And moving things in the heavens
For your earthly good.
The silence of God means
He has already met your every need.
The silence of God means
He loves you and He knows
What you are going through.
The silence of God means;
He has lifted every burden,
And worked all things out just for you.
The silence of God means…..
When He speaks you will know!

Help That You Need:

There are several ways a person can journey through their grief. Let the person know that in order to move forward and understand their losses, it helps to participate in the group sessions or individual counseling.

Bereavement and grief counseling groups provide support to people who have experienced any type of loss. Although there are specific groups for people who have had a loved-one die due to homicide, suicide, cancer, or miscarriage; a spouse or partner, parents, children, or pets.

Grief is grief and a loss is a loss; to categorize them depends on the facilitator of the group. The bottom line is, these groups' help individuals learn how to accept the loss of any kind, honor the memory of their loved-one, and adjust to life after a loss.

Please note individual counseling and grief group support may take time, depending on the root of each person's problem. Healing and restoration cannot begin until the root cause of the issues is recognized and dealt with.

Individual Counseling: Involves one on one support from a counselor. Upon arrival of the bereaved, the counselor will do a brief assessment to determine the best way to help the bereaved. During that time, regular scheduling of appointments will take place if needed. The bereaved will be asked to enter into an agreement with the counselor that everything discussed during their meetings are confidential and if for some reason that agreement is broken, counseling sessions will end.

Counseling sessions are set and agreed upon by the counselor and bereaved. If there are no breakthroughs, the bereaved may be asked to attend a grief support group. Often times it helps to be around others and to hear their story; it lets the bereaved know they are not alone. If the bereaved does not want to attend a grief support group, the other option would be to refer to an outside Christian counselor who may be able to devote more time. This is done so that counselors may assist others who are in need as well, and can give quality time to each person.

Grief Support Groups: Consists of no more than 10 people per group. The days, hour and time of the grief support group are set by the facilitator. The purpose of having a small group is to create a safe intimate environment conducive for people to share their deepest feelings. Most people connect better in small groups because they feel comfortable.

- Closed Groups: No one else can come and be a part of the group once the program has started. Having a closed group makes individuals feel comfortable with bonding and sharing a bit more.

- Open Support Groups: Are open to the community and anyone is allowed to drop in and out at any time. Often times there is not a set number per group.

They usually meet once a week at the same place and time. Open groups are good for those who need a bit of encouragement every now and then as they journey through their loss. There should always be a facilitator present; two people facilitating if possible would be great. It makes it easier for dividing the participants into groups. A facilitator is there to give direction and help set the tone of the group by making sure everyone has adequate time to express what's in their heart. The participants are the ones that make the group flow by sharing with each other. Activities within the group depend on how the facilitator has it arranged. Therefore, each grief support group may differ a bit.

Grief Camps: This usually takes place during the summer time either on a weekend or possibly for an entire week; there again it depends on the facilitator. The camp will be free of charge to each camper, but will require a complete application. It would be wise to set the number of participants that will be received, along with the deadline date to submit applications.

This is a big event and may involve networking with other churches or organizations to help with funding, counseling and other needs. The camp is divided into peer groups, accommodating children (5-11), teenagers (12-18) and parents/ guardians and individuals. The campers will be involved in multiple activities; along with age-appropriate grief sessions. The idea is for families to heal together; a chance to get away and breathe, by changing the atmosphere. It offers the family time to process the loss and gives them a chance to meet others with similar circumstances. At the end of each day, everyone will come together in one location, with all the leaders and team members. It is at that time where campers will have the opportunity to share how participating in the camp has or has not helped them journey through their grief. At the end of the Grief Camp, all the campers will take home a dedicated project in memory of their loved one or of their other loss.

Artmustherapy: My personal creation which involves a free-flowing form of creative art combined with prayer and music. No prior art classes are needed. This can stand alone as a grief group session or can be incorporated in with the main grief support group. Artmustherapy is designed to help people, acknowledge, deal and release their inner feelings that may not be expressed through verbal communication. It has been proven that this form of group offers amazing healing to the inner man and promotes a meaningful way of finding peace. At the end of the session, each person will take with them their art masterpiece in remembrance of their loved-one.

Sympathy Cards: Sympathy cards can be sent out to families and individuals for death dying and other losses. It's good to have one card for grieving and one for sympathy; keep it short and uplifting. You can make it personable from the entire church with the pastor's signature if your congregation is small enough to allow all the members to sign it. The other alternative could be to send the card out to the bereaved the following week after the loss with the signature of the pastor and church family.

Phone Support: Offers prayer, listening and communication to the bereaved. There may be times when a bereaved cannot participate in a grief support group or perhaps may be at home experiencing some type of anxiety, loneliness or depression. To receive a phone call from someone to let them know you care may be just the thing they need.

As the Bereavement Ministry grows you can create your own form of support groups to meet the need of the people within the church and community.

7 SELF-CARE FOR THE BEREAVED

Psalm 139:13-14

For you formed my inward parts; you covered me in my mother's womb. I will praise you for I am fearfully and wonderfully made; marvelous are the works and that my soul knows very well.

3 John 1:2

Beloved, I pray that you may prosper in all things and be in health, just as your soul prospers

Philippians 4:13

I can do all things through Christ who strengthens me.

As the bereaved person begins to heal, allow them to be gentle with their self and to avoid harsh judgment. Some may tell them that they are moving too fast or too slow, but continue to remind them that there are no timetables to grieving. Let the natural healing process of the body, mind and soul work; do not try to hurry them along. Laughter is good for the soul and will come as the bereaved moves forward; sometimes guilt creeps in because they often feel as if they are being disrespectful to their loved one that died or don't deserve to be happy due to their past circumstances. Let them know it is okay to enjoy life.

Permission to Backslide: Sometimes after a period of feeling good, the bereaved may find themselves back in the old feelings of extreme sadness, despair, or anger. This is often the nature of grief; sometimes up and down. It may happen over and over for a time. It happens because as humans we cannot take in all of the pain and the meaning of death or any loss at once. So, we let it in a little at a time what our mind and heart can handle. Explain to the bereaved that everything they are experiencing is natural.

Time: Encourage time alone and time with others who they can trust and who will listen when they need to talk and not be judged.

Rest: Stress is a killer and in a time of grief the stress factor may rise. Relaxation, exercise, nourishment, diversion may need to increase a bit; hot baths, afternoon naps, a trip. Often times a person may feel the need to volunteer to help others who have experienced a loss. Note, if the loss is a death of a loved one, the person who wants to volunteer should wait at least 6 months. Grief is an exhausting process emotionally; a person may need to replenish oneself. Allow the bereaved to follow what feels as healing to them and what connects them to the people and things they love.

Security: At times there may be financial burdens before and after a loss. The bereaved needs time to put things back in some kind of order. If they are employed going back to work may be a bit difficult. Perhaps the loved-one was the total support therefore, the bereaved will need to find security in taking care of themselves.

Hope: Finding hope and comfort from those who have experienced a similar loss may come through grief support groups. Sharing stories or just being in the room knowing some things that helped other people and realizing how they have recovered or are recovering can make a big difference.

Caring: The expressions of caring from others can be very helpful to a person grieving. Even though you may feel uneasy and awkward because you don't know what to say; listening or perhaps sitting quietly in the room with the bereaved could help more than you know. It's good to let them know someone is there and they are not alone.

Goals: For a while, it may seem that much of life is without meaning to the bereaved, therefore goals often times are helpful. It provides something to look forward to. Talk to the bereaved about visiting with a friend, and the following week a movie, and perhaps a weekend trip to get away from surroundings.

Small Desires: As the bereaved begins to get out and experience small desires; remind them that God does give us the desires of our heart even after a loss. Remind them of the body's need for nutrition and rest. Remind them to listen to the messages their body gives them. As they return to what may feel normal there may be moments of painful realization of the loss and resentment toward the world and others may creep in. Unexpressed words or tears can cause lumps in their throats: anger held inside can cause a headache or upset stomach.

Remind them to not underestimate the healing effects of spending time with family and friends, and as the pain of grief becomes less, it is okay to take a walk on the beach, enjoy a laugh, and eat their favorite meal. All of that is the beginning of God restoring their pleasure back into their life.

8. OPERATION EXCELLENCE
(FORMS)

Romans 8:38

"For I am persuaded that neither death nor life,

Nor angels nor principalities

Nor powers, nor things present nor things to come,

Nor height nor depth,

Nor any other created thing

Shall be able to separate us from the love of God

Which is in Christ Jesus our Lord."

(Sample Bereavement Volunteer Letter) We Would Love Your Help! We are all blessed to be a blessing to others. Are you willing to hold a hand, sing a song, help with office work, plan a special event, address envelopes, feed a pet, make a speech, bake a cake, prepare a meal, reach out with a phone call, listen to cherished memories, pat a shoulder, give a hug, touch a heart? Whether you want to work directly with an individual or families, or in another role, you can make a difference in someone's life. Volunteer; let someone see you smile because "a smile can change one person's life." If God has placed in your heart a passion for those who grieve, please consider becoming a (Your name here) Volunteer. Volunteers are a critical part of the ministry. Though Christ Jesus, you can make a difference in the life of others.

Bereavement volunteers need to complete a Volunteer Application Form that includes references, personal questions & answers, signed confidentiality statement, signed liability statement, signed code of conduct, and a media release (Facebook, Google, Twitter.)

Teens ages 13-17 may volunteer in supported settings and are required to have a signed Parent/Guardian's consent. Volunteers who will have direct contact with loved ones must be aware and agree that they are responsible for maintaining their own personal health. And in no way by any means, hold the Bereavement Ministry responsible should they become sick for any reason.

(Sample Liability Letter) As Bereavement Ministers and volunteers, there may be times when entering into adverse situations and circumstances may take place. The Bereavement Ministry does not provide liability insurance for the protection of individual, groups, organizations, businesses, spectators, or others who may participate in the bereavement ministry.

The individual, group, organization, business, spectator or other, does hereby release and forever discharge The Bereavement and its ministers, board, members, jointly and individually from any and all actions, causes of actions, claims, demands for any loss, damages, or injury now or hereafter.

I understand I am responsible for my own belongings, and valuables, such as jewelry and electronic devices. The Bereavement Ministry will not be responsible for any lost or missing items. (Signature and date of both parties needed)

(Sample Confidential Statement) Bereavement Ministers and volunteers frequently observe and receive confidential information concerning loved-ones and individuals. Confidentiality is based upon the right of privacy; it is the ethical obligation of the Ministers and volunteers and is necessary to create effective trust.

Bereavement Ministers and volunteers are required to ensure confidentiality and privacy with regard to history, records, and discussions about the bereaved.

No information about an individual or family who is or have received counsel through (Your name here) Bereavement program will be offered or provided to anyone without a signed release of information form from that particular individual or family member.

Copying of records or removal of records is strictly prohibited.

Only within bereavement meetings can and should information be shared about families, and individuals. This is not a violation of confidentiality as all Ministers and volunteers are equally bound to honor that information as confidential outside of this setting.

When a volunteer suspects that a bereaved may be at risk of harm to self and/or others, that information must be communicated to a Bereavement Minister as soon as possible.

Any suspected child abuse or neglect, however remote the suspicion, must be reported to ministers as soon as possible. The professionals' legal obligation to report suspected child abuse supersedes the loved one or individual's right to confidentiality.

Violation of confidentiality may be grounds for disassociation from the bereavement part of the ministry.

I have read this Confidentiality Agreement and understand that it is my responsibility to comply with it, and I agree to do so. (Signature and date of both parties needed)

(Operation Excellence Form) Positive behavior is a key expectation for participating in the bereavement ministry. Positive behavior reflects trustworthiness, respect, responsibility, fairness, caring and encouraging those who grieve.

As part of the bereavement team, you are expected to fully participate, follow all program guidelines and behave appropriately to ensure a high-quality learning experience and ensure the safety of individuals, families and their loved-one.

Theft, vandalism, the use of illegal drugs and alcohol are prohibited. Those engaged in illegal activities will be turned over to the proper authorities.

Inappropriate sexual behavior and behavior that violates the rights of others, particularly when the behavior is disrespectful as regards to a person's gender, race, age, sexual orientation, religion, national origin, disability or appearance will not be tolerated.

I agree not to use offensive language, gestures or actions that will hurt others.

Ministers/ Volunteers dress should always be neat and appropriate, for the occasion.

Our primary consideration is to provide a safe, secure, trustworthy environment for all participants ministered to through the bereavement ministry.

I have read and agree to abide by subject matters outlined in the

Operation Excellence Form.

(Sample Volunteer Form)

1. Name:

2. Address:

3. Phone:

4. Mobile:

5. Email:

6. Birthday:

7. Emergency Contact:

8. Previous /Current Volunteer Experience (Please enter where you volunteered and the dates):

9. Education/Special Training (Please list any training or experience relevant to death, loss, grief, bereavement):

10. Special Interests/Hobbies:

11. Do you have any medical conditions that we need to be aware of? Yes   No   Please list:

12. Are you a U.S. Veteran? Yes   No Please list branch:

13. Please list recent reference (Preferably other volunteer jobs or professional references):

I Authorize the Bereavement Ministry to check my references

14. Do you speak any languages other than English? Yes   No   if yes please list:

15. Are you currently employed? Yes   No

16. What type of volunteer ministry do you desire? (Circle all that apply) (Administration) (Community Liaison) (Patient Care) (Errands) (Shopping) (Music) (Bereavement) (Fundraising) if other please list:

17. Has anyone close to you died in the past two years? Yes/No   If yes, who?

18. How did you hear about volunteering with (Your name here) "Bereavement?"

19. Have you had a loss of any kind other than the death of a loved one within the past 2 years? (Example, pet, home, job, limbs, etc.)

Yes No If yes, please list:

20. How many hours a week do you feel you can commit to volunteer? (Enter a number between 0-40)

21. What times of day are you available to volunteer?

22. Please Circle (Mornings) (Afternoon) (Evenings) (Weekdays) (Weekends) other:

23. Are you allergic to anything? Yes No List, if any.

(Sample Ministry Opportunities, Not limited) Here is a list of the things that your church can provide. As time goes on, you may add to or take away from the list. Each ministry is different.

Serve as a prayer partner

Direct patient and family care opportunity

Visiting with patients to provide companionship

Providing respite and support services for the caregiver (if trained in that field)

Assist with grief and bereavement support groups for adults or children

Helping with follow-up calls to check on families who have recently lost a loved one

Support for individuals and families who are grieving from everyday life issues.

Community Support Outreach

Music

Cooking

Children and adult summer grief camp assistant

(Sample Consolidated Bereavement Assessment) This form serves as a two-fold purpose for the use of the initial assessment when the loved one is dying or has died. This form also serves as a person that has suffered any type of loss. It is important because it allows the Bereavement Ministry to have insight on how the family or individuals are coping with the death of their loved-one and other losses.

The bereaved or loved-one is (check which applies) actively dying, already deceased, grief for other losses.

The bereaved or loved-one is in need of (check all that applies) a volunteer, social work, pastoral, financial support, Grief Support Group, individual counseling.

Name of bereaved/loved-one:

Relationship:

Address:

Phone / Home/ Mobile:

Emergency Number:

Name of loved-one:

If deceased, date of death:

If living, has the love one been diagnosed with a terminal illness: Yes/No

Name, address and phone number of Primary Care Physician and or healthcare facility:

Have you chosen a Funeral Home? Yes/No, if yes, list name, address and phone number.

If no, do you need help choosing a place, making arrangements, or financial support?

Is there a living will? Yes/No

Do you have Power of Attorney? Yes/No

Do you have an Advance Medical Directive? Yes/No

If no, do you need help in that area? Yes/No

Are you in need of the following: Grief Support Group, individual counseling, volunteers, social work, financial support, pastoral?

If checked, please explain your need:

Grief for Other Losses:

Individual - Briefly explain loss:

Contact (home/work/mobile phone:

Other contact information:

Address:

Assessment Begins Here Check all That Apply:

Reason for visiting: Complete assessment, Pastoral Counseling, Crisis Intervention, Code Blue, death & dying, grief & bereavement, trauma/emergency, emotional support, or could not get information

Faith: Methodist, Catholic, Baptist, Presbyterian, Jehovah's Witness, Buddhist, non-denominational, other, or could not get information

Importance of faith: High, low, medium, not sure, saved, not saved, or could not get information

Support Network: None, poor, good, excellent, family supportive but out of town, church, close family support, support of friends, husband, wife, other

Bereaved Relationship with Loved-One and others: Little dependency, strong dependency, uncertain, intimate & long lasting, conflict, no dependency, respectful, caring, hostile, angry.

Bereaved Role in Care of Loved-One: Case Manager, sole care provider, no communication, caregiver /Nurse, Pastor

Bereaved Preparation for loss: Actively prepared, prepared, some readiness, unprepared, clear acceptance, full denial

Coping Mechanisms: Avoidance, Distraction, Escape, Drugs, Alcohol, Food, Withdrawal, Fair, Good coping , Poor coping, Need additional help, Urgent help needed, Normal, Anger, Eating and sleeping, Stronger person through it all, Bitter, Irritation, Denies any feelings, Self-blaming, Occasional outbursts, Other

Other Life Crisis: Job loss, Relocation, Other Deaths, Divorce,

Abandonment, Loss of limbs, Strong financial issues, Poor health, Imprisonment/Probation, Loss of home, Loss of belongings, Other

This next area of the assessment is important because it gives the ministry a bit of knowledge into the family history of the bereaved. Check all that apply.

Ongoing marital or family discord, History of substance abuse, Abusive behavior, History of mental health, Religious/Spiritual dynamics, Cultural dynamics, Children in the home/ ages

Living arrangements, Personal health issues, Difficult with decision making, Inability to tolerate stress, History of suicide, other

Grief Minister's Signature, Date Complete.

9. POWERFUL GRIEF SCENARIOS

This section is written to give you a bit of insight on a few scenarios that a person may encounter. Remember grief covers all aspects of life, and no one person will grieve the same way. These scenarios are based on a combination of events. Names of people places and things have been changed.

Scenario 1 - Received a call from the hospital that there was a young lady that requested to talk to a chaplain. While driving to JHC, I beginning to pray and ask Holy Spirit to show me what to do once I arrive. Upon my arrival, as I approach the patient's room, there in the bed lay this young girl, perhaps in her 20's. As I looked to my left, there was another young girl sitting in a chair doing something on a laptop computer.

Important Note: (Always make sure that when entering a patient's room that you notice the entire surroundings, it can give you a bit of understanding about the patient)

As I introduced myself to the patient and made mention that I was there on behalf of her call, the patient acknowledged my present. The lady on the computer asked the patient if she wanted to be alone, and the patient stated yes, so the young lady left the room. Our conversation began with me asking the patient her name and why she was in the hospital. Even though you may already know the patient's name, asking the question often times can be a way to break the silence/ice, or heaviness that may be in the atmosphere. The patient stated her name and continue to say, "I am in the hospital because I gave birth to twins and they both died".

The patient continued to speak and said: "I was holding one child in my arms and he was alive, but then the second child came out dead, and when I looked back at my first child he died within seconds afterward."

The patient was sitting there in the bed with no real sign of human emotions or life. She stated that she had only one question and that was, what happens when babies die? She wanted to know what she was supposed to do now because her life was planned around her having the children. (The entire time I am listening carefully so I do not say the wrong thing once I begin to talk.) The patient continued to say that she had decorated the room and had everything ready to bring her children home. We continued to talk and she shared with me that she could not talk to the father of the children because she believed he was only with her because she was pregnant. I ministered to the patient by explaining to her that we do not have all the answers as to why certain things happen in our lives the way that they do. I assured her that God is a good God and that Jesus loves her. I continued to let her know that God is not out to cause her pain. I explained to her to be absent from the body is to be present with the Lord. Therefore, we must believe that her children are now with the Lord.

At that moment, that answer I believe gave her comfort and a sense of pain as she began to weep. It was explained to her that she has life and that her life can and will in time, move forward. It was explained to her that it was okay to cry, but in order to make it through her grief, she would need the help of the Lord. The patient was not saved, had no real knowledge of Christ. At that moment the patient when asked the question if she wanted to be saved, stated yes and believed, and gave acceptance to Christ as her Lord and Savior.

To minister to someone who has had a child die can be very challenging if you have never had that type of loss yourself. The only thing you can do is try to make a connection using the word of God. Often times it is not as easy and each situation is different. In this patient's case, she was seeking answers which made ministering to her a bit easy. In this scenario, the patient will need follow-up and a connection with a strong bible-believing church.

Scenario 2 – The patient has been admitted to the hospital from a motorcycle accident; he is approximately 27 years of age. He has a large supportive family; some who have a church affiliation.

The patient has his own business as a Computer Repairman as well as an Ice Cream delivery business.

This visit was a normal routine visit. Upon entering the patient's room, he is in the bed with both legs in a cast and bandages around his mid-section.

(C) Chaplin (P) Patient

Conversion begins as the chaplain enters the patient's room.

C- Hello how are you?

P- On the phone "Hey man I'll call you back; someone just walked in my room.

C- Hi, I am Mary, one of the Chaplains on duty.

P- (Laughs and says) Ok, this is a joke right? My auntie sent you here didn't she?

C- (Smiles) No, I am here on behalf of the hospital and today is your day.

P- (Still laughing) Okay, so my auntie or my mom called the hospital and told you to come here.

C- No, I am checking on patients on this floor and happen to come into your room. I actually walked by your room, then turned around and decided to come into this room. We visit patients all the time and offer spiritual support to them and their families.

P- Ok, cool, but are you sure my family didn't send you?

C- Yes, I am sure; so what's going on with you?

P- (Looking disappointed) Well, I did something really stupid.

C- What did you do?

P- Well, I got really upset about something and jumped on my motorcycle to go see a guy about the problem I knew nothing about. As I was going around the curve in the road, I lost control of my bike. I had two choices, either turn the wheel and go off the road into some bushes and everything or to let the bike fall on the road and cause danger, not just to myself but others. So, I choose to go into the bushes and here I am.

C- (with compassion) Sorry that you had an accident, at least you are okay, a bit banged up, a few broken ribs, two broken legs, but it could have been worse. It seemed God spared your life; if you don't mind me asking, what made you so mad?

P- (Puzzled) You know what, that is the fourth time someone has said to me that God has spared my life.

C- Are you a Christian?

P- Nope! I am not a Christian, but my auntie and mom are. (Pause) A lot of women in my family are who I am around a lot; can't seem to get away. I know! I know! I'm going to hell because I'm not saved.

C- Do you want to be?

P- No.

C- Okay

P- (Laughs) What? Is that all you're going to say? You mean you're not going to point your finger at me like most preachers do and tell me I am going to burn in hell? Preach fire and brimstone?

C- (Smile, but serious) No; it's a choice and you choose not to be saved.

P- Well, I just came out of prison. I have been locked up since I was 15 years old for robbery. No, I didn't get saved in jail like most people do. But I wrote a book about my life and want to help other people; (looking at the chaplain) know what I mean? And since I've been out, I've started my own business. That is what made me so mad. I have an Ice-Cream truck business. The guy that was driving my truck did not show up for the deliveries. (Pause) No, it's not an illegal business (he laughs) I know that's what you're thinking, but, I was headed to his house to see what the problem was. And the truth is (paused) it was not going to be, umm, well, let's just say it was not going to look good. So, I guess the accident had to happen. You know you're a pretty cool minister, you need to meet my auntie; she's a minister too.

C- Sounds like you had a rough start, but you are on the right track now. But we should never allow someone to make us so angry. Because in the long run, or short run in your case, it only hurts you.

P- Yeah, I've been told that before too. I know God as you call Him.

(Pause) But I'm going to say, umm, the Creator who creates everything has looked after me for a long time. I've had three motorcycle accidents before this one.

C- Well, you have been blessed; life spared yet again. Can I leave some information with you? (Pulling out literature)

P- (Laughs) I'm not gonna read it, I promise you; it will be a waste of your time.

C- (Smiles) Listening and sharing with you is not a waste of time, trust me. I'm going to leave this with you; it's a gospel track. You can read it to someone else, or give to them; but it is yours to have.

P- (Takes the track) Bet, do you have a card or something I can give my auntie?

C- (Smiles) Yes, (gives card) you have a great night and I will check on you tomorrow.

P- Ok, yeah, hey, do you have a computer?

C- Yes

P - (Excited) I bet it needs some work right? Will you look over there on the table and take one of my cards, and if you need some work done, give me a call.

C- Sure, (getting a card) okay, have a good night.

P- You do the same.

In this scenario, it was very obvious that the patient had an issue with God. He was very open and honest about who he was, and his relationship with Christ. Sometimes it's good to just have a conversation with the patient without trying to win them to Christ right away. Often times if we just let the love of Jesus be glorified in us, we can be a more effective witness.

By the Chaplin not preaching hell, fire, and brimstone, it caught the patient off guard from what he was used to hearing. Which in my opinion created an atmosphere for a seed to be planted, and someone else to water it.

Scenario 3 - Received a call from EC that there was a bad car accident, and the family needed a Chaplain. Upon arriving at the EC, the charge nurse began to give a briefing that the man driving his car was hit head-on by an oncoming vehicle. Upon impact, the man was thrown through the windshield. **(Problem)** The man had brain damage and the doctors stated that chances of his survival were very slim. **(Assessment)** The young man had a large family and it appeared that each one of them, along with friends, were in the lobby waiting for the results. They were very loud and distraught which caused others around them to be a disturbed. **(Help Provided)** Since the family was so large and many friends were there as well, finding the main person in charge was the key thing to do. It appeared that the fiancée of the man dying was in charge and the family had a lot of respect for her. Even though she was stressed, she was still able to be of assistance. Therefore, the immediate family was gathered together into a private room which had enough space.

The ability to communicate was good and we were all able to wait for the doctor's result. Upon waiting, it was stated that the man who was fighting for his life was the person with the family that held everyone together. He was the one that everyone looked up to and went to when they had issues; he was always there for the family. Now with his life hanging in the balance the family was falling apart. There was a best friend that was there among the family that stated he and the patient made a pack with each other a long time ago that if anything was to happen with either of them that one would step in and take care of the other one's family. So he encouraged the family that whatever the outcome would be, they would all be okay.

In short, upon the death of the patient, the family asked for prayer. Instead of the chaplain praying, the best friend prayed.

I believe what helped this family the most was that the best friend was there and he was able to offer a comfort to the family that the chaplain was not able to give, which is okay. When ministering to those who grieve, we as ministers should always have a listening ear to what Jesus is saying and the leading of Holy Spirit.

Scenario 4 - This scenario is what I call an **"Extra Ordinary Woman";** it truly demonstrates **Grief God's Way.**

I received a call from my dearest "bffffffffff" as she so defines our friendship. As I listened to her broken heart's cry, my eyes filled up with tears and I begin to weep in silent as she began to tell me, through her stuttered words her story.

This woman's husband had just died. He was on his way from the doctor's office to get his medication and while driving had a heart attack. Now, this situation was very personal to me because first, she was my best friend and second I was the Minister that married them.

In short, I arrived at her home to help make funeral arrangements. But this heart-broken woman that I spoke to and prayed with over the phone, had now tapped into the presence of the Lord and Jesus is literally carrying all her grief. I saw with my eyes, witnessed and participated in the purest form of Isaiah 53:4 come to life, where it says; "He bore our grief and carried our sorrows". Wow! What a marvelous encounter.

During the seven days I was there, when visitors came to her home to offer their condolences, she encouraged them and prayed with them.

I watched as people came to her home thinking that she would be so distraught, feeble-minded, broken, tattered and torn; but *they* ended up healed, set free, and delivered from their own brokenness.

Baptism with Holy Ghost and fire, evidence of speaking in tongues poured into some who visited; it was amazing. I saw and experienced in Holy Spirit's presence pour His fresh anointing into this woman every day. And I was thankful for the freshness of His presence falling on me too.

When the spirit of grief would come to overtake her, I saw it leave immediately. At the funeral, this woman stood tall, as people came into the church for the home going celebration, she greeted them one by one and thanked them for coming. There were times when tears would fall from her eyes, but she let it be known that those tears were tears of joy because she knew that her husband was a Christian; he was saved and with the Lord. As Jesus bore her grief, this woman did not miss a beat, she stood in front of the entire church and gave the most powerful, encouraging, moving, tribute with humor to her beloved husband that I had ever seen, which touched the hearts of the people and compelled some to change their lives. Today, she is still going strong and Jesus has truly carried her grief.

As you continue to speak life to those you minister to that are hurting; may Father God continue to expand your mind and impart more wisdom, knowledge and revelation of His word into you so that you will be continually blessed to be a blessing to others and build up His kingdom.

Never forget that as leaders in your community or church that everyone has a different grief experience. Jesus is love and His word tells us through love and kindness, have I drawn thee.

Be patient with a person as they journey through their grief. Show them the compassion that you yourself would want, if and when you are grieving.

Remember grief comes in many ways, forms, shapes, sizes, and colors. Never forget that yes, God put doctors here for us, but Jesus The Christ is the ultimate healer.

May the love of Jesus overwhelm and fill you with so much joy that it overflows out of you into everyone you meet.

Have an awesome forever....

ABOUT THE AUTHOR

Dr. Christine Rice Slocumb is an author, writer, and speaker, with a doctorate in ministry, grief counseling, and chaplaincy.

Since 1999 she has ministered to and has transformed the lives of patients, families, and individuals who experience traumatic emotional traumas, and those who need crisis interventions and end of life care; or perhaps just a listening ear.

She and a co-worker developed a grief support group program "Artmustherapy" that adventurously shows how the advantage of creative arts combined with a certain category of music along with prayer can make a major impact in the lives of those who grieve.

She is the published Author of *Keeping It Real When Infidelity Strikes.* (Publisher, Skills of Success & Associates, Inc. 2014.)

Not only did writing the words on paper set her free, but since then, *Keeping It Real When Infidelity Strikes has* helped many others who have been struggling with everyday life issues.

Her messages through her writings are inspiring, empowering and healing for the soul. Her books embrace a unique style of poetry and songs along with scripture which leads into each chapter that captivates your attention. She writes from a "keeping it real heart" that invites you in; which makes you feel as if you are an audience of one.

She speaks to both Christian and secular audiences on diverse topics relating to everyday life issues.